Veiled or Ye Chameleons as Pets

A Complete Owner's Guide

Including Information on Baby Veiled Chameleons, Female
Veiled Chameleons, Chameleon Cage Setup, Breeding,
Colors, Facts, Food, Diet, Lifespan and Size

Published by Atticus Publications

© 2014 Atticus Publications

Printed and bound in Great Britain by Lightning Source.

Foreword

This book is designed to provide you with answers to your most pressing questions about veiled chameleons. Here you will learn everything from the history of the species to facts about what to feed veiled chameleons and how to care for them. Because this book is written in a clear and easy-to-read fashion, you will find it a joy to read. By the time you finish this book you will have a good idea whether or not the veiled chameleon is a good choice for you and your family – you will also have a firm foundation of knowledge to prepare you for owning and caring for your chameleon.

Acknowledgements

I would like to thank my friends and family for their love and support while I worked through this project. Special thanks to my wife for encouraging me to turn my passion into a book.

Table of Contents

Chapter One: Introduction

The veiled chameleon is one of more than 150 species of chameleon, though it is easily one of the most recognizable. Known for the crown-like casque on top of its head, the veiled chameleon is a very unique and attractive species. The interesting appearance of this animal, along with its ability to change colors, is one of the things that makes it so popular as a pet. In fact, veiled chameleons are quickly rising to the top of the list as one of the most popular species of pet chameleons.

If you are looking for a unique and interesting pet –

something other than a cat or dog – the veiled chameleon is definitely something you should consider. While these pets are not recommended for inexperienced reptile owners, veiled chameleons can and often do thrive in captivity with proper care. It is important to realize, however, that chameleons have very specialized needs so you will need to do plenty of research before you bring one home.

That is where this book comes in! In this book you will find all of the information you need to get started in preparing for your own veiled chameleon as a pet. Here you will learn the basics about the species including how they compare to other pet chameleons. In reading this book you will receive a wealth of knowledge about the care and keeping of veiled chameleons, including tips for decorating their cage, creating a healthy diet, and even breeding them. By the time you finish this book you will not only have a good idea whether this is the right pet for you, but you will also be well on your way in preparing to care for one.

Useful Terms to Know

Ambient Temperature – the temperature of the environment

Arboreal – living primarily in trees

Camouflage – the use of coloration to disguise the animal, making it less visible to predators

Casque – a hard, helmet-like ridge on the top of the head

Cloaca – the chamber that opens through the anus; used for both reproduction and excretion

Ectothermic – referring to an animal that cannot regulate its own body heat; body heat is regulated by the temperature of the environment

Endemic – indigenous (native) to a specific region

Gravid – referring to a female bearing eggs

Hatchling – a newly hatched chameleon, a baby chameleon

Herpetology – the study of reptiles and amphibians

Insectivore – an animal that subsists primarily on insects

Oviparous – an animal that lays eggs which develop outside the female's body before hatching

Prehensile Tail – a tale that is capable of grasping or wrapping; acts as an additional appendage

Sexual Dimorphism – having obvious physical differences between the male and female sex of the same species

Tarsal Spur – a spur found on the back of the rear feet of male veiled chameleons; used during breeding

Chapter One: Introduction

Terrarium – a cage for keeping reptiles and amphibians

Tetrapod – a vertebrate animal having four limbs

Thermoregulation – the ability of an animal to maintain a certain body temperature despite the surrounding temperature being different

True Chameleon – species belonging to the family Chamaeleonidae in the order Squamata

Vent – the opening from the cloaca; anus

Chapter Two: Understanding Veiled Chameleons

If you have ever owned a pet reptile before, you will know that they are very different from "traditional" pets like cats and dogs. Before you can decide whether a veiled chameleon is the right pet for you, take the time to learn the basics about this species. In this chapter you will learn basic information about the veiled chameleon including their appearance, size, history and more. You will also learn some pros and cons about veiled chameleons as pets so you can decide if they are right for you and your family.

Chapter Two: Understanding Veiled Chameleons

1.) What Are Veiled Chameleons?

The veiled chameleon is also known as the Yemen chameleon because it is native to an area of Western Asia called Yemen – the official name of the country is the Republic of Yemen. This species can also be found in parts of the United Arab Emirates and Saudi Arabia. The veiled chameleon is sometimes referred to as an "Old World" chameleon because they are only naturally found in countries that are part of the "Old World" – that is, parts of the world that were known prior to contact with the Americas. These chameleons are also sometimes called "true" chameleons.

Veiled chameleons are just one of several species of chameleon that are kept as pets. What makes the veiled chameleon one of the most popular species, however, is the fact that it tends to be fairly hardy in captivity. Veiled chameleons also tend to be a little more aggressive and territorial than other chameleon species, so special care should be taken when keeping these animals as pets. Chameleons in general are not recommended for inexperienced pet owners, especially for those who have never owned a reptile before.

2.) Facts about Veiled Chameleons

The veiled chameleon is a species of reptile belonging to the family Chamaeleonidae. This reptile is one of many species of chameleon, known for its ability to change color. Males of the species are primarily green in color with yellow, brown or blue stripes but these colors may change according to the animal's mood and stress level. Females of the species are typically all green in color with some white markings. When a female is gravid, however, her color darkens to a deep green and she develops blue or yellow spots – the vibrancy of these markings may vary depending on the lizard's mood. Both sexes exhibit a large casque – a hard, helmet-like formation – on the top of the head.

Not only do male the female veiled chameleons exhibit a difference in color, but they are also very different in terms of size. The fact that males and females of the same species exhibit such obvious differences is referred to as sexual dimorphism. While females of the species typically grow only 10 to 14 inches (25 to 35.5 cm) in length and have a weight between 3.2 and 4.2 oz. (90 to 120 g), male veiled chameleons grow to 17 to 24 inches (43 to 61 cm) long and weigh between 3.5 and 7 oz. (100 to 200 g). Another difference in the sexes is the tarsal spur found on the back of the hind legs in males of the species – this spur is present at hatching but grows as the chameleon matures.

Like most chameleons, the veiled chameleon is an arboreal species so it spends most of its life in the trees. These reptiles can be found using their prehensile tails as a fifth appendage, aiding in its climb through the forest. Veiled chameleons also have rounded eyes that swivel back and forth – in fact, the chameleon is capable of looking both backwards and forwards at the same time. In contradiction to chameleon myth, however, the veiled chameleon does not have a sticky tongue. Rather, the long tongue of this species has a special muscular structure on the end that enables it to grab its prey. Using its tongue, the veiled chameleon snatches up unsuspecting insects as they pass by while the lizard lies patiently in wait.

The veiled chameleon is technically an omnivore, which means that it derives its sustenance from both vegetable- and meat-based food sources. For the most part, however, these chameleons are insectivores which means they primarily eat insects. If little food is available the veiled chameleon will eat leaves, blossoms and fruit. Another interesting fact about the veiled chameleon is that they do not drink standing water – they only recognize droplets of water on leaves as a water source. In captivity, a chameleon that is only offered standing water will likely dehydrate.

a.) How Chameleons Change Color

While some species are known for changing color more than others, all chameleon species are able, to some degree, to alter their coloration at will. Different species have been known to exhibit all sorts of colors including green, brown, black, red, white, pink, orange, yellow, turquoise, purple, and everything in between. In many cases, color change in chameleons is a reaction to changes in temperature or other environmental conditions – it can also be used as camouflage and as a means of social signaling.

The importance of color changes in chameleons varies by circumstance. For example, a chameleon might indicate its physiological condition or its intentions to another chameleon using its color. Darker colors are linked to anger and aggression, displayed in the hopes of intimidating predators or potential competitors. During mating, however, males tend to exhibit lighter colors when courting a female. Some desert-dwelling chameleons change their color as a means of thermoregulation – darkening in the morning to absorb heat and changing to a lighter color later in the day when it gets hot.

The method by which chameleons change their color is very interesting – it involves the use of specialized cells called chromatophores. These cells contain pigments in the cytoplasm and they are housed in several layers beneath a transparent outer skin. The chromatophores located in the uppermost layer contain yellow and red pigments while those in the middle layer contain blue and white. Chromatophores in the lower layer contain a dark pigment called melanin which controls the reflection of light. The concentration or dispersion of these specialized cells affects the intensity of each color.

b.) Summary of Facts

Scientific Name: *Chamaeleo calyptrus*

Classification: true chameleon, family Chamaeleonidae

Country of Origin: Yemen (also United Arab Emirates, Saudi Arabia)

Chapter Two: Understanding Veiled Chameleons

Habitat: primarily in forested portions of the mountains

Diet: omnivorous, though primarily insectivorous

Size (male): 17 to 24 inches (43 to 61 cm) average

Size (female): 10 to 14 inches (25 to 35.5 cm)

Weight (male): 3.5 to 7 oz. (100 to 200 g)

Weight (female): 3.2 to 4.2 oz. (90 to 120 g)

Color (male): bright green with yellow, brown and blue spots/stripes

Color (female): overall green, some white markings; develop dark green color with blue/yellow spots when gravid

Unique Characteristics: casque on the head, prehensile tail, swiveling eyes

Sexual Dimorphism: males are larger and more colorful, have spurs on the back of the hind feet

Sexual Maturity: 6 to 8 months

Lifespan: average 7 years

3.) History of Veiled Chameleons

The oldest known species of chameleon is the *Anqingosaurus brevicephalus*, now extinct, which lived during the Middle Paleocene era in China. Other early chameleon fossils have been collected from Germany and Kenya, dating back to both the Lower and Upper Miocene eras. Though fossils have only been found for chameleons dating back to about 60 million years ago, it is likely that these animals have been around for much longer.

It is possible that chameleons share a common ancestor with iguanids and agamids from more than 100 million years ago. Judging by fossil evidence, chameleons were once more widespread across the globe than they are today. Today, nearly half of all extant chameleon species are found in Madagascar with others found throughout mainland Africa and the surrounding area.

4.) Types of Chameleons

The veiled chameleon is one of many different species of chameleon. Though there are more than 150 species of chameleon, only a few are recommended and popular as pets. <u>In this section you will find information about other types of chameleons kept as pets including the following</u>:

Carpet Chameleon

Fischer's Chameleon

Jackson's Chameleon

Meller's Chameleon

Oustalet's Chameleon

Panther Chameleon

Carpet Chameleon

The carpet chameleon (*Furcifer lateralis*) is native to the forests and woodlands of Madagascar. Like the veiled chameleon, this species is also primarily arboreal. Carpet chameleons are a small species of chameleon with males

growing up to 9 inches (22.8 cm) on average. These
chameleons have dark green bodies with stripes on the
throat and lips – females of the species may exhibit a wider
range of colors and patterns. Though hardy in captivity,
these chameleons are timid as pets.

1: Carpet Chameleon (Furcifer lateralis)

Fischer's Chameleon

Fischer's chameleon (*Kinyongia fischeri*) is found in the
mountainous regions of Tanzania and Kenya. There are
several different species similar in appareance to the
Fischer's chameleon and there is some debate regarding
whether they are all one species or not. Fischer's chameleon

is a shy and secretive species that reaches an average length between 9 and 11 inches (22.8 to 28 cm), though they are capable of growing up to 15 inches (38 cm).

2: Fischer's Chameleon (Kinyongia fischeri)

Jackson's Chameleon

Also known as the three-horned chameleon, Jackson's chameleon (*Trioceros jacksonii*) is found in the cool, humid regions of Kenya and Tanzania in Africa. This species typically reaches about 12 inches (30 cm) in length and they are easily identified by the saw-tooth shaped crest on their heads. This species tends to do well in captivity, though they require a much higher humidity than some chameleons and they need cooler temperatures at night.

The Jackson's chameleon is bright green in color, some with traces of blue or yellow coloring on the body.

3: Jackson's Chameleon (Trioceros jacksonii)

Meller's Chameleon

Also known as the giant one-horned chameleon, Meller's chameleon (*Trioceros melleri*) is the largest species of chameleon found on the African mainland. These chameleons can grow up to 24 inches (61 cm) in length, though some have been recorded at lengths of 30 inches (76 cm) or more. Meller's chameleons are a stout-bodied species of chameleon with a stubby tail that measures only one third the length of its body. In captivity, these chameleons have been known to be a little aggressive toward humans,

17

though others are timid. Wild-caught specimens tend to have parasite problems and often do not do well in captivity, though captive-bred specimens are much hardier as long as their specific habitat requirements are met.

4: *Meller's Chameleon (Trioceros melleri)*

Oustalet's Chameleon

Also known as the Malagasy giant chameleon, Outstalet's chameleon (*Furcifer oustaleti*) is a very large chameleon endemic to the island of Madagascar. This species of chameleon has been recorded at a maximum length of 27 inches (68.5 cm) and it is often considered the largest species of chameleon. Oustalet's chameleons can be found in a wide-ranging habitat in Madagascar where they feed largely on insects but have also been known to eat small birds and mammals.

5: Outstalet's Chameleon (Furcifer oustaleti)

Panther Chameleon

The panther chameleon (*Fucifer pardalis*) is found in the tropical forest regions of eastern and northern Madagascar. This species of chameleon reaches an average length around 17 inches (45 cm), though females of the species are usually smaller. Panther chameleons vary in coloration by locale with some exhibiting bright blue colors while others are red, orange or green. Males of the species tend to be more colorful than females – females are usually brown or tan with hints of pink or orange color. Out of all the pet chameleon species, the panther chameleon is one of the most adapted to captivity and generally does well around people with proper care.

6: Panther Chameleon (Fucifer pardalis)

Chapter Three: What to Know Before You Buy

Bringing any new pet into your home is a big responsibility and not a decision that should be made lightly. Now that you have learned the basics about what veiled chameleons are, you may be curious to know more about what they are like as pets. In this chapter you will learn some useful information about veiled chameleons as pets including information about licensing requirements, the costs associated with caring for them, and the pros and cons of veiled chameleons as pets. By the time you finish this chapter you should have a good idea whether this is the right pet for you and your family.

1.) Do You Need a License?

You may already be aware that certain countries require cat and dog owners to license their pets – but what about non-traditional pets? Reptiles like the veiled chameleon fall into an entirely different category than dogs and cats, so the licensing requirements and restrictions may vary from one area to another. Before you go out and buy a veiled chameleon (or two) you should be sure that it is legal to have one where you live. In this section you will learn the basics about licensing requirements for reptiles like the veiled chameleon in the U.S., the U.K., and other areas.

a.) Licensing in the U.S.

When it comes to licensing animals other than cats and dogs in the U.S., you generally do not have to worry unless it is a native or endangered species. There are no federal regulations regarding the keeping of reptiles like the veiled chameleon as pets, but certain states may have restrictions. For example, in the state of Maryland you may be required to obtain a Captive Reptile & Amphibian License if you plan to keep certain reptiles as pets. According to state regulations, however, this permit is only required for species native to Maryland – as long as the reptile is not native to the state, no permit is required.

You will find similar requirements in other U.S. states, but be sure to check with your local council to make sure that you do not require a permit to keep veiled chameleons where you live. The only other legislation you may need to consider is the Endangered Species Act which closely regulates the sale and keeping of endangered species. Fortunately, the veiled chameleon is neither a native U.S. species nor an endangered species, so you are unlikely to require a permit or license to keep them in the U.S.

b.) Licensing in the U.K.

In the U.K. there are no licensing requirements for the keeping, selling, or breeding of reptiles, including the veiled chameleon. The only exceptions may be for reptiles that are considered dangerous or endangered species. You should be aware, however, that there is legislation in place to ensure the proper care and keeping of pets. The Animal Welfare Act was passed in 2006 which outlines the basic rights of animals and the responsibility of pet owners to provide a suitable environment and diet for their pets and to meet their needs for companionship, shelter and safekeeping. Though this act does not apply specifically to reptiles, it is something you should keep in mind.

c.) Licensing in Other Countries

Licensing requirements for other countries outside the U.S. and the U.K. may vary, depending where you live. In Australia, for example, the National Parks and Wildlife Act of 1974 protects wild reptiles and amphibians. Australia also requires an Animal Keeper's License for owners of pet reptiles, but only if they are native species. In other countries the requirements are likely to be similar – licenses or permits may be needed for native species but, as long as the veiled chameleon is not considered native, you are unlikely to need a permit to keep one.

2.) How Many Should You Buy?

As is true for most Old World or "true" chameleons, the veiled chameleon is best kept individually. The veiled chameleon has a bit of a reputation for being more aggressive and territorial than some other chameleon species, so it would be unwise to keep more than one of them in the same cage – particularly two males of the same species. Even in the wild, veiled chameleons tend to avoid each other except in cases of breeding. The only exception is in raising juvenile veiled chameleons – young chameleons may be raised together for a short period of time until they grow large enough to need their own cage.

3.) Can Veiled Chameleons Be Kept with Other Pets?

Because veiled chameleons are semi-aggressive and very territorial, it is unwise to keep them in the same cage as other reptiles or amphibians. Though veiled chameleons are primarily insectivorous in the wild, in captivity they may view smaller reptiles like anoles as prey if they are kept in the same cage. Ideally, your veiled chameleon should have a cage all to himself.

4.) Ease and Cost of Care

Another thing you need to consider before you decide to bring a veiled chameleon home is whether or not you have the financial means to care for one. In addition to buying the chameleon and his cage, you also need to consider ongoing costs for food, supplements and utility costs for lighting and heating. In this section you will find a detailed overview of both the initial costs and monthly costs associated with keeping veiled chameleons as pets.

a.) Initial Costs

The initial costs for keeping a veiled chameleon as a pet include those costs which you must cover prior to bringing your chameleon home. These costs include the cost of the cage, cage decorations, heating and lighting, and other equipment – you also have to factor in the cost of the chameleon itself. Below you will find a description of each of these costs as well as a table displaying the total for initial costs.

Purchase Price – The purchase price for veiled chameleons varies depending where you buy and what age the chameleon is. A juvenile chameleon is likely to cost less than an adult and, if you buy from a pet store, you are likely to pay more than you would at a reptile trade show or from a breeder. For the most part, you should expect to spend between $30 and $100 (£19.50 - £65) for a veiled chameleon.

Cage – Again, the cost for your veiled chameleon's cage will vary depending on the size and materials you choose. The main point of variation is in the materials from which the cage is constructed – a glass aquarium is likely to be more expensive than a screen enclosure but, in some areas, it is the best option. You will read more in Chapter Five about finding the right cage for your veiled chameleon. In addition to materials, you also have to think about the cost – for a wire mesh cage measuring 24x24x48 inches (61x61x122 cm), you can expect to pay between $80 and $120 (£52 - £78). A glass enclosure, on the other hand, may cost between $150 and $300 (£97.50 - £195).

Cage Decorations – Specific information about recommended cage decorations for veiled chameleons can be found in Chapter Five. For the sake of budgeting, however, you should know that you will need to purchase a variety of live plants (though plastic will work in a pinch) as well as basking rocks and branches. You should expect to pay between $50 and $150 (£32.50 - £97.50) for cage decorations.

Heating and Lighting – Maintaining the proper heat and humidity in your veiled chameleon cage is extremely important, so you do not want to skimp on these costs. To keep your chameleon's cage within the proper parameters you will need to buy reptile heating lamps, UVB bulbs for day lighting and light fixtures to hold the bulbs. You may also want to buy an under-tank heating pad to keep the substrate warm. To save money, you may want to buy your light fixtures at a home improvement store rather than purchasing them from a pet store – they will be just as useful but half the price. Plan to spend $50 to $200 (£32.50 - £130) for heating and lighting in your chameleon cage.

Other Equipment – Other equipment you may need to get your veiled chameleon cage set up might include an automatic timer for your lights, a spray bottle or dripping source for water, a lid for your cage (if it doesn't come with one) as well as food bowls. The estimated cost for these items (which will vary depending what items you buy and their quality) is about $20 to $100 (£13 to £65).

Cost Type	Estimated Cost Range
Purchase Price	$30 to $100 (£19.50 - £65)
Enclosure	$80 to $300 (£52 - £195)
Tank Decorations	$50 to $150 (£32.50 - £97.50)
Heating and Lighting	$50 to $200 (£32.50 - £130)
Other Equipment	$20 to $100 (£13 to £65)
Total:	$230 to $850 (£150 to £553)

b.) Monthly Costs

The monthly costs for keeping veiled chameleons as pets include those costs which you will need to cover on a recurring basis. These costs may include food, supplements, substrate, veterinary care, and repairs or replacements for the cage. Below you will find a description of each of these costs as well as a table displaying the total for monthly costs of keeping a veiled chameleon.

Food – Because veiled chameleons are primarily insectivorous, you will need to keep a wide variety of live insects in stock. You can buy small containers of crickets, meal worms and waxworms at your local pet store but it would be much more economical to order in bulk online or to raise them yourself at home. You will only be feeding your chameleons 3 to 4 times per week once they are an adult and the amount of food your chameleon eats will vary. For the sake of budgeting, plan for a food cost of $40 (£26) per month to keep a variety of insects.

Supplements – To ensure that your veiled chameleon gets all the vitamins and minerals he needs, you should dust your feeder insects with powdered supplements at least once a week. You will read more about the specific supplements your veiled chameleon needs in Chapter Five but, for the sake of budgeting, plan to spend about $10 (£6.50) per month on supplements, keeping in mind that one container will likely last more than a month.

Substrate – The type of substrate you use in your veiled chameleon cage is up to you. Some reptile owners prefer to use some kind of synthetic reptile carpeting while others use moss or bark. Your chameleon will spend most of his time climbing around in branches, so do not feel like you need to spend a lot of money on substrate. With weekly cleanings, you will likely spend about $15 (£9.75) per month on substrate if you go with bark or moss.

Veterinary Care – Though veiled chameleons do not require vaccinations or routine check-ups in the same way that dogs and cats do, you should have an exotic vet available in case you need him. Keep in mind that exotic vets will charge more for their services than traditional vets that only see dogs and cats – you should plan to pay between $50 and $80 (£32.50 to £52) per visit. Budgeting for one visit per year, this cost averages to about $5 (£3.25) per month.

Repairs/Replacements – Over time you will need to replace or repair certain parts of your veiled chameleon cage. If you are using live plants in your cage, you will need to account for plants dying once in a while as well as the need to replace branches if your chameleon eats the leaves off of them. You should also think about the cost of replacement bulbs for your lighting and repairs for chips, cracks or tears in the cage. Budget for about $10 (£6.50) a month to be safe.

Cost Type	Estimated Cost Range
Food	$40 (£26)
Supplements	$10 (£6.50)
Substrate	$15 (£9.75)
Veterinary Care	$5 (£3.25)
Repairs/Replacements	$10 (£6.50)
Total:	$80 (£52)

5.) Pros and Cons of Veiled Chameleons

Making the decision to bring a new pet into the house is not one that should be taken lightly, especially with a non-traditional pet like the veiled chameleon. Before you decide to buy one you should take the time to learn everything you can about them – this includes the advantages and disadvantages of keeping them as pets. Below you will find a list of pros and cons for veiled chameleons as pets:

Pros for Veiled Chameleons

- Can be kept in an all-inclusive enclosure
- Very interesting to keep as pets, especially with color-changing abilities
- Unique appearance makes the veiled chameleon a non-traditional pet
- Habitat requirements can largely be automated (timers for lights, thermostat for heating, etc.)
- Sexual dimorphism means that if you prefer a smaller chameleon, you can simply choose a female
- Do not require a great deal of interaction or stimulation from owners

Cons for Veiled Chameleons

- Fairly aggressive compared to other chameleons
- Cannot be kept in the same cage with another chameleon or other reptiles
- Requires a fairly large cage that will take up significant space in the home
- Generally not recommended for inexperienced reptile owners
- Not considered a friendly pet, not particularly good for children
- Requires specialized care in regard to heating, lighting and humidity
- Primarily follows an insectivorous diet which will require feeding of live insects

Chapter Four: Purchasing Veiled Chameleons

Now that you have learned the basics about veiled chameleons and what is involved in caring for them, you may be ready to decide whether or not this is the right pet for you. If you have already made this decision, you may be ready to move on to thinking about purchasing a veiled chameleon. In this chapter you will learn the basics about how to go about finding veiled chameleons for sale and how to choose one that is healthy. Purchasing a veiled chameleon is a process that should not be rushed, so take your time in reading and following the tips in this chapter.

1.) Where to Buy Veiled Chameleons

If you have decided that a veiled chameleon is the right pet for you, you still need to think about a few things before you buy – primarily, where you are going to get the chameleon. While you may be able to find veiled chameleons at your local pet store, you need to consider whether this is really the best option. Below you will find tips for buying veiled chameleons in both the U.S. and the U.K. so you can be sure you get one that is healthy.

a.) Buying in the U.S.

Stopping in to your local pet store is a good place to start in buying a veiled chameleon in the U.S. Even if the pet store does not have any chameleons, you may be able to ask the store owner for recommendations for breeders in the area. If the store does carry chameleons, think carefully before buying one – if you buy from a pet store rather than directly from a dealer, you don't know exactly where the chameleon is coming from. You also don't know the conditions in which it was raised or what diseases it may have been exposed to in the pet store.

If you want to increase your chances of bringing home a chameleon that is healthy, consider buying from a breeder or reptile dealer. To find local breeders and dealers, check the ads in your local paper or perform a search online. Keep an eye out for reptile trade shows that may be coming to your area or consider asking around at local pet stores for information regarding local dealers. As a last resort, you can look for private sellers on websites like Craigslist who may be looking to rehome their chameleons for a small fee.

b.) Buying in the U.K.

In the U.K., your options for buying a veiled chameleon are similar to in the U.S. While you may be able to find them at your local pet store, stop and consider whether you might not be better off buying from an experienced breeder or dealer. If you choose to buy from a breeder or dealer, make sure to ask plenty of questions regarding the breeding process used and the quality of the breeding stock. This goes for purchasing a veiled chameleon from a breeder or dealer in the U.S. as well – the more careful you are in buying your chameleon, the less likely you are to bring one home that has medical problems.

2.) How to Select a Healthy Veiled Chameleon

While taking the time to select a reputable breeder or dealer is important in bringing home a healthy chameleon, it is not the only thing you can or should do. Once you know who you are getting your chameleon from, you should take the time to look at the chameleons available so you can pick one that looks healthy. If you can, try to buy a juvenile chameleon so that you can raise it with a healthy diet, thus minimizing its risk for health problems down the line. When checking out potential breeders and dealers, follow these tips for selecting a healthy chameleon:

- Make sure that the chameleon is captive-bred, not wild-caught
- Check to be sure that the chameleon's eyes are bright and free of discharge – chameleons that keep their eyes closed during the day are likely sick
- The chameleon's legs should be straight – bent or bowed legs are an indication of metabolic bone disease
- Check to see if the chameleon can get a good grip on branches – if it appears weak, it might be sick

- The coloration of the chameleon should be bright – if the chameleon's skin looks dull or patchy, it is likely sick
- Look for signs of mouth rot (green or cheese-like growths around the mouth)
- Check for signs of scratches or bruises on the chameleon's body
- Look around the cage for signs of diarrhea – the cage and the chameleon's cloaca should be relatively clean

Note: If you come across a chameleon that is being kept poorly, try to resist the urge to "rescue" it – the chameleon is likely already sick or stressed and will only be more difficult for you to care for.

Chapter Five: Caring for Veiled Chameleons

Caring for a veiled chameleon is much different than caring for a cat or a dog. While "traditional" pets like cats and dogs are able to roam free through your home, veiled chameleons require a special cage that is designed and maintained to suit their needs in regard to heating, lighting and humidity. In addition to a suitable environment, your veiled chameleon also requires a healthy diet that meets his basic nutritional needs. In this chapter you will learn how to create a suitable environment for your chameleon and how to provide for his nutritional needs.

1.) Habitat Requirements

Veiled chameleons have very specific requirements in terms of habitat so, before you buy one, you need to be sure that you can meet your chameleon's needs. Unlike cats and dogs, chameleons need a cage where they will spend all of the time that you are not handling them. This cage should, ideally, be made to simulate the chameleon's natural environment through decorations, temperature, humidity levels and more. In this section you will learn how to design and set up the ideal cage for your chameleon.

a.) Basic Cage Requirements

Because veiled chameleons grow to be fairly large, up to 24 inches (61 cm) long for males, their cage needs to be large as well. If you do not provide your chameleon with an adequately large cage, he is likely to become stressed and may also suffer from injuries by bumping into the cage walls. The minimum recommended cage size for veiled chameleons is 24x24x48 inches (61x61x122 cm). That is, the cage should be at least 24 inches (61 cm) wide and deep with a height of at least 48 inches (122 cm).

These cage dimensions are the minimum recommended for veiled chameleons – it is always better to go bigger than the minimum recommended size, however. Think about the fact that your chameleon will be spending almost his entire life in this cage, so it should be large enough for him to live in it comfortably. If you are going to go with a larger cage, you shouldn't feel the need to make it much more than 36 or 48 inches (91 to 122 cm) wide – height is the more important factor. Veiled chameleons are an arboreal species so they will need plenty of room to climb around on branches in their cage.

If you are purchasing your veiled chameleon as a juvenile, you may be able to get away with a smaller cage to start with. Juvenile chameleons can be housed in a cage measuring about 16x16x30 inches (40.6x40.6x72 cm) until they reach a length of about 8 inches (20.3 cm). At this time, however, they should be transferred to the larger cage you will keep them in for the remainder of their life. There is no harm in keeping your juvenile chameleon in a larger cage to start with, but it is not recommended that you keep him in a smaller cage once he reaches a length of 8 inches (20.3 cm).

In addition to the size of your chameleon's cage, you also have to think about the materials from which it is made. The two most common materials for reptile cages are mesh vivariums and glass terrariums. For the most part, mesh vivariums are preferred by chameleon owners because they provide air flow that cannot be accomplished in a glass tank. Glass tanks tend to accumulate moisture which can lead to fungal infections and respiratory issues in veiled chameleons, so they are best avoided if possible. The only time you should consider using a glass terrarium for your veiled chameleon is if you live in an area that is consistently cold – a glass tank will be easier to regulate temperature-wise than a mesh vivarium.

A third option for housing your chameleon exists – you can also build your own cage. To build your own cage, you can construct a frame out of non-toxic wood or PVC pipe and enclose it with fine mesh or PVC-coated hardware cloth. When building your own chameleon cage it is important that you have a tight-fitting lid so your chameleon cannot escape. You should also be careful about the type of mesh or screen you use – if the gauge is too wide your chameleon could get a limb caught but, if it is too small, it could obstruct airflow into and out of the cage.

b.) Lighting and Heating Requirements

The next step in preparing your veiled chameleon cage is to incorporate adequate heating and lighting. Veiled chameleons require their cage to be within certain temperature ranges – ranges which change from day to night. During the day, your cage should be within the range of 80° to 90°F (26° to 32°C) while, at night, it should only drop by about 10° to 15°F (5° to 10°C). In addition to the daytime temperature, you also need to provide a basking spot for your chameleon that reaches at least 95°F (35°C). The basking area can safely reach a temperature of 110°F (43°C) without having any negative effects.

To keep your chameleon cage within the proper temperature range, you should use a combination of heating pads and heat lamps. Using reptile heating pads under the substrate in your chameleon's cage will help to increase the ambient temperature, but heat lamps will be more important for helping your chameleon to thermoregulate. Depending on the size of your chameleon's cage, you may need to use several heat lamps. In order to provide your chameleon with a basking area, at least one of the heat lamps should be positioned so that a basking area or perch is situated only about 6 to 8 inches (15 to 20 cm)

45

below. As an alternative, you can also create a shelf in your chameleon's cage and set up a heat rock.

While heat lamps are important for establishing and maintaining ambient temperature in your chameleon's cage, they are not the only type of lighting you should use. UVB lighting is also essential because it helps chameleons to absorb and utilize important vitamins and minerals like calcium – if your chameleon doesn't receive adequate exposure to UVB light, he may be at a higher risk for developing metabolic bone disease (MBD). Avoid using bulbs that combine a heat source with UVB lighting because chameleons are able to regulate body heat and UVB exposure separately. Just as you should position a heat lamp about 6 to 8 inches (15 to 20 cm) above a perch for basking, you should do the same for at least one UVB bulb.

You should plan to keep the UVB lights on in your chameleon's cage for about 10 to 12 hours each day. You will need to do a bit of experimenting to see how many and what combination of bulbs you can turn off at night to maintain an ambient temperature within the proper nighttime range. Depending on the climate where you live, you may not need any nighttime heat source to maintain the proper temperature. If you do, however, make sure to find a heat lamp designed for night time or use a ceramic heater instead. If you use a ceramic heater, place it outside the cage to eliminate the risk of burns.

c.) Setting up and Decorating the Cage

The most important decoration element to use in your veiled chameleon cage is plenty of branches for climbing. The easiest way to incorporate branches is to place small trees or shrubs directly in the cage – some good options include ficus, hibiscus and dracaena. Live plants are a great option for the chameleon cage because they are natural and authentic – they also keep growing, providing your chameleon with constant places to hide. Additionally, you should also provide plenty of medium-sized vines that your chameleon can use to perch on and to travel around the cage as he pleases.

As for the floor of your chameleon's cage, how you cover it is not particularly important. You may choose to line the bottom of the cage with reptile carpet or a bark or moss substrate, but there is really no need to cover the floor at all if you prefer not to. There are benefits to leaving the floor of your chameleon's cage bare. Not only will it be easier to clean, but it is also less likely to accumulate moisture which can contribute to the growth of bacteria and fungus.

d.) Cage Cleaning/Maintenance Tips

To maintain the humidity in your chameleon's cage, and to provide him with drinking water, you will need to mist the cage several times a day. The easiest way to do this is to use a spray bottle of warm water, misting the cage for 1 to 2 minutes twice a day. It is important that you use warm water for this and that you keep in mind the fact that water cools as it hits the air. Therefore, you may need to fill the bottle with fairly hot water to ensure that it stays warm once it is sprayed. To test the water, spray it into your hand at a distance of about 12 inches (30.5 cm).

Other options for providing your chameleon with water include installing an automatic mister, using a bowl of water with an air stone, or creating a dripping water source. Automatic misters can be fairly expensive, so spraying the cage yourself twice a day is usually the preferred option for many chameleon owners. You can easily make a dripping water source by filling a plastic cup with water and making a pin hole in the bottom. Water dishes outfitted with an air stone to move the water may attract the attention of a chameleon, but it is not the best option.

In terms of cleaning your chameleon's cage, you should remove solid feces as often as possible. Leaving the bottom of the cage bare makes this much easier – it also means that you can wipe the cage out with a pet-safe cleaner to disinfect and sanitize it. If you choose to use bedding in your chameleon cage, remove and replace it on a weekly basis to prevent the accumulation of waste and moisture.

2.) *Feeding Veiled Chameleons*

In the wild, veiled chameleons are omnivorous – their diet consists mostly of insects but they have also been known to eat some vegetation. In captivity, your chameleon's diet is going to be less varied than in the wild, so there are certain precautions you must take to ensure that he gets the nutrition he needs. In this section you will learn the basics about your veiled chameleon's nutritional need and receive tips for formulating a healthy diet.

a.) Nutritional Needs

The key to meeting your veiled chameleon's nutritional needs is to provide him with a varied diet. While a veiled chameleon can survive on a diet of crickets alone, it is better to provide him with a variety of different insects because different insects provide different nutrients. Crickets, for example, are high in protein while certain types of worms provide dietary fat. If you don't give your chameleon a variety of different insects, his diet may become overloaded with one nutrient and deficient in another.

The most important vitamins and minerals your veiled chameleon needs include calcium, phosphorus, vitamin A and vitamin D3. While some of these nutrients may come from your chameleon's diet, many chameleon owners recommend the use of reptile supplements. These supplements typically take the form of powder that can be dusted on feeder insects before you offer them to your chameleon. When using nutritional supplements, it is important to strike the right balance between using too little and too much. If you use too little, your chameleon could be at risk for metabolic bone disease while, if you use too much, he could face other health problems.

Recommended schedule for supplementation:

- Gut-loading of insects, daily
- Dusting insects with calcium/vitamin D3 supplement, 2 to 3 times a week
- Dusting insects with broad vitamin/mineral supplement, once a week

*Note: Some veterinarians recommend avoiding supplements that contain Vitamin A for reptiles, recommending beta-carotene instead.

b.) Types of Food for Chameleons

Veiled chameleons eat a wide variety of insects in the wild, but you are only likely to have access to certain types. Some of the insects recommended for veiled chameleons include the following:

- Crickets
- Meal worms
- Wax worms
- Silkworms
- Moths
- Flies

- Locusts
- Roaches
- Butterworms
- Grasshoppers

When feeding your veiled chameleon insects, it is important to be careful where they come from. Never feed your chameleon insects that you gather from your backyard because you do not know what type of pesticides and other chemicals the insects may have been exposed to. You should also take care to gut-load your feeder insects before you offer them to your chameleon. All this involves is feeding the insects healthy foods like collard greens, squash and mustard greens. When your chameleon eats the crickets, the nutrients they gathered from their own food will benefit the chameleon as well.

Though insects will fulfill the majority of your chameleon's nutritional needs, you may also offer your chameleon small amounts of fresh vegetables from time to time. Some vegetables your chameleon may enjoy include butternut squash, kale, zucchini, collard greens, red pepper, and dandelion greens as well as bits of fruit like apple and blueberries. Your chameleon may also eat some of the leaves from the plants in his cage, so make sure you choose non-toxic plants for decoration.

c.) Feeding Frequency and Tips

The frequency with which you feed your chameleon will change depending on his age. Juvenile chameleons should be fed more frequently than adults – in fact, you may want to make sure some kind of food is always available. When your chameleons reach maturity, taper off their feeding until you are only doing it 3 to 4 times per week. During each feeding, you should only offer as many insects as your chameleon will eat during a 30 to 45-minute time period. Remove any uneaten insects from the cage so they do not make a mess.

Follow these tips for feeding your chameleons:

- If your chameleon shows little interest in food, try increasing the temperature in his cage for a few days

- Use crickets that are only as large as the width of your chameleon's head

- Note that it is not unusual for a chameleon to eat as many as 15 or 20 large crickets in one feeding

- You may consider offering a commercial insectivore diet, though not all chameleons show any interest this type of food

- Avoid larger winged insects because they can be difficult for your chameleon to digest

- Always feed your chameleon during the day when he is most active

- If you are worried about insects escaping from the cage, you can consider using a feeding cup

- Keep in mind that offering free-roaming insects will encourage your chameleon to get more exercise in chasing them down

3.) Handling Your Veiled Chameleon

Veiled chameleons are not the type of pet that you will spend a lot of time handling – at least not in the same way you would a dog or a cat. While some species of pet chameleon are fairly calm or even timid around humans, veiled chameleons have the potential to be a little aggressive. It may take some time for your chameleon to get used to you, and you shouldn't expect him to ever become fully tame. In fact, if you handle your chameleon too much, he may become stressed.

Chapter Five: Caring for Veiled Chameleons

Follow these tips when handling your chameleon:

- Understand that your chameleon is unlikely to enjoy being held – in fact, he would be perfectly happy if you never touched him at all

- Avoid the temptation to attribute human feelings to your chameleon – just because he crawls up your arm doesn't mean he is tame and a nip to your finger isn't a "love bite"

- Limit the time you spend handling your chameleon to 5-minute sessions no more than 1 or 2 times per week

- Be gentle when removing your chameleon from the cage and place him on your arm – let him crawl on you rather than trying to hold him in your hands

- Consider wearing gloves to protect yourself from bites and scratches

- Avoid making sudden movements – not only could you knock your chameleon off, but he might view it as an attack and bite you

Keep in mind that temperament varies from one chameleon to another. Some may let you handle them and they might even seem to enjoy it, while others would rather be left alone. Observe your chameleon closely to gauge his reaction and if he appears stressed, do not force him to come out of the cage.

Chapter Six: Breeding Veiled Chameleons

Breeding chameleons at home is no easy task – it takes a great deal of research and preparation in order to do it correctly. Once you do achieve a successful breeding you also have to go through the process of caring for and raising the babies. If you are curious about what it might be like to breed your veiled chameleons, or if you are seriously considering doing so, you will find the basic information you need to know in this chapter. Here you will learn the basics about breeding chameleons as well as tips for encouraging breeding and caring for the young.

Chapter Six: Breeding Veiled Chameleons

1.) Basic Breeding Info

Before you can breed your veiled chameleons, you should cultivate a basic understanding of how they breed. Veiled chameleons are oviparous breeders which means that they lay eggs rather than giving birth to live young. This species can reach sexual maturity as early as 4 to 5 months, though it is generally recommended that you do not breed a chameleon younger than 6 months. In many cases, the size of the chameleon is a better indication of sexual maturity than age – veiled chameleons can be safely bred once they reach a size of 8 to 12 inches (20 to 30.5 cm).

If you aren't sure whether the female is ready for mating or not, you can always introduce her briefly to the male to see how she reacts. If the female turns black and starts gaping her mouth, or if she hisses and rocks back and forth, she is not ready for breeding. If the female is ready, however, she will retain her neutral coloration and may walk slowly away from the male, enticing him to follow her. If the female shows signs of not being ready for breeding, remove her from the cage immediately and keep her separated from the male for a while longer.

Chapter Six: Breeding Veiled Chameleons

When you are sure that the female is ready for breeding, you will introduce her into the male's cage rather than the other way around. After breeding, if conception occurs, the female will go through a gestation period of 1 to 3 months. The length of the gestation period may vary, but the female will generally lay her eggs after 30 to 40 days. After 20 days, it is recommended that you start to provide nesting material so that the female does not become egg bound.

The average clutch size for veiled chameleons varies greatly – they can lay anywhere between 12 and 80 eggs. For the most part, however, the average size of a veiled chameleon clutch in the wild is between 12 and 20 eggs. In the wild, veiled chameleons that produce very large clutches generally only live to produce a few clutches because the act of laying so many eggs can be extremely taxing on the animal's body. After the eggs are laid, they will be incubated for between 150 and 200 days before hatching.

2.) The Breeding Process

Because veiled chameleons are fairly aggressive and territorial, you should only introduce the male and female when you intend for them to breed. In many cases, chameleons breed readily in captivity, but you have to make sure that the conditions are right. You cannot simply bring a female into the male's cage and expect the two to breed – you must wait until the female displays signs that she is ready for breeding. In most cases, she will develop blue patches along the sides of her body.

When the female is ready to breed, introduce her to the male's cage and give them some time – be sure to stay close by, however, in case they get aggressive. After the male chases the female around the cage a big, copulation will take place. Fortunately, veiled chameleons make it very obvious when they have conceived. Within minutes of a successful mating (when the female is inseminated) she will turn black with bright yellow and green spots. When this happens, you know it is time to remove the female from the male's cage.

After the female is successfully inseminated, she will carry the eggs for a gestation period lasting between 30 and 40 days on average. By day 20, you should start to prepare nesting materials so that they are available when the female is ready to lay her eggs. If proper nesting materials aren't available, the female may refuse to lay her eggs which could become very dangerous for her health. The ideal nesting box for a veiled chameleon consists of a large 5-gallon (19 liter) bucket or tub filled with 6 to 12 inches (15 to 30.5 cm) of moist soil or a blend of sand and peat moss.

Observe the female closely as she approaches the end of her gestation period. When she starts to appear very restless and wanders around the cage in search of her nesting area. Over a period of several hours, the female will dig a deep hole in the substrate then she will turn and deposit her eggs. Once the eggs have been laid, she will bury them completely. After the female lays her eggs, you can remove the nesting box and dig up the eggs to transfer them to an incubation box where they will develop over the next 150 to 200 days before hatching.

3.) Raising the Babies

To construct an incubation box for your veiled chameleon eggs, use something similar in size to a plastic shoebox. Fill the box with Perlite or slightly moistened vermiculite and align them in the substrate, spacing them 1 inch apart. Veiled chameleon eggs are fairly small and oval-shaped with a tough white skin. Infertile eggs may be dented or yellow – they will also not have blood vessels in them that you may see in the fertile eggs if you hold one up to the light in a dark room.

Cover the incubation box with a lid and drill a small hole into two opposite corners to facilitate a little air exchange. Keep the box in a dark room, maintaining a temperature around 75°F to 85°F (24° to 29°C) during the day and allowing it to drop to around 68°F (20°C) at night. It will take at least 150 days for the eggs to hatch and when they are almost ready, you will notice that they start to "sweat". The eggs will also begin to cave in – a day or so later, they will hatch.

Once your veiled chameleons hatch, you can house the hatchlings in a 10-gallon (38-liter) aquarium with a screen top. Keep the temperature between 88° and 95°F (31° to 35°C) during the day and allow is to drop to 75° to 80°F (24° to 26°C) at night. Decorate the tank with small live plants to give your hatchling chameleons plenty of space for climbing – the hatchlings are also likely to eat the leaves which is good for them. You can safely keep 6 or 7 hatchlings in one cage at a time so, depending on the size of the clutch, you may need several of these cages.

Feed your hatchling chameleons pinhead crickets – as many as they will eat. Make sure to dust the crickets with calcium supplements as well to help the hatchlings form strong, healthy bones. Spray the cage every other day to keep the humidity up and to provide the baby chameleons with drinking water. Once the hatchlings reach 2 months of age you should separate the sexes, keeping them in cages whether they will not be able to see each other. At this time, it is generally safe to send your hatchlings off to their new homes.

Chapter Seven: Keeping Veiled Chameleons Healthy

Providing your veiled chameleon with a healthy diet and a clean habitat will go a long way in keeping him healthy. There are, however, other factors which may contribute to your chameleon falling sick if you aren't careful. In this chapter you will learn about the diseases to which veiled chameleons are prone – you will also receive information about the causes, symptoms and treatment for those diseases so you know how to handle them. In this chapter you will also receive tips for preventing illness.

Chapter Seven: Keeping Veiled Chameleons Healthy

1.) Common Health Problems

While providing your veiled chameleon with a clean environment and healthy diet goes a long way in keeping him well, there may come a time when your chameleon gets sick. Your chameleon's chances of making a full recovery decrease every day you wait to provide treatment, so it is important that you are able to identify diseases when they occur and start treatment right away. The key to making this possible is familiarizing yourself with the conditions likely to affect veiled chameleons so you can recognize the symptoms right away, make a diagnosis and get your chameleon started on treatment.

Some common conditions affecting veiled chameleons in captivity include:

Bacterial Infections	Kidney Failure
Dehydration	Metabolic Bone Disease
Edema	Respiratory Infection
Egg Binding	Stomatitis
Intestinal Parasites	Stress

Bacterial Infections

In reptiles like chameleons, bacterial infections may take many forms. For the most part, bacteria are opportunistic agents – they may be present in the cage for long periods of time without doing any harm but, if the animal becomes stressed, sick, or injured the bacteria may become active. The key to preventing bacterial infections in your veiled chameleon is to keep his cage clean and to ensure that he doesn't suffer from stress.

Two of the most dangerous bacterial infections known to affect captive reptiles are septicemia and ulcerative dermatitis. Septicemia is a systemic bacterial infection which is often preceded by trauma, parasitism or stress due to poor husbandry. Common signs of septicemia include respiratory distress, lethargy, convulsions and loss of coordination. Reptiles suffering from this condition should be isolated (if they are not already) and treated with antibiotics.

Ulcerative dermatitis, also called necrotic dermatitis, is most commonly seen in reptiles kept in unhygienic conditions. Damp bedding allows fungus and bacteria to reproduce and they may enter the bloodstream through ingestion or open cuts and wounds. Common symptoms include ulcers, lesions, and discharge and treatment requires antibiotics.

Dehydration

As was mentioned earlier in this book, if you only provide your chameleon with a bowl of drinking water, he is unlikely to recognize it as a water source. In the wild, chameleons drink from droplets of water on leaves and branches, so if you only give them a bowl of water they may become dehydrated. Unfortunately, the signs of dehydration are easy to overlook so it is possible that the problem could become advanced before you even notice.

Some common symptoms of dehydration in chameleons include loss of appetite, sunken eyes, lethargy and, eventually, death. Keeping the humidity levels in your chameleon's cage at the proper level will help to prevent dehydration, but you also need to mist the cage frequently (several times a day) so that your chameleon has water to drink. If your chameleon becomes dehydrated to the point where he is too weak to drink water that is offered, you need to seek immediate veterinary care.

Edema

This condition is characterized by swelling in certain areas of the body as a result of fluid accumulation. In most cases, edema is a symptom of an underlying condition such as hypoproteinemia, lymphatic blockage, renal disease or inflammation/sepsis. Edema is most likely to occur in chameleons when there are not enough proteins in the bloodstream because proteins are what help to keep fluids within the blood vessels.

Some common symptoms of edema including swelling of the joints, throat, and neck region. Edema is gravity-dependent, so it is most likely to manifest in the lower areas of the body or areas that hang down when the chameleon is perched. Treatment for edema typically requires veterinary care because the primary cause of the condition must be identified in order to determine the right treatment. Prevention for edema involves proper use of supplements (too little may cause deficiencies while too much might lead to edema) and adequate hydration.

Egg Binding

In female chameleons, egg binding is an incredibly dangerous – and often fatal – condition. Like most reptiles, chameleons reproduce by laying eggs. In cases where the female is unable to or unwilling to lay the eggs at the appropriate time, she becomes "egg bound." The longer the eggs stay in the female's body, the more nutrients they will absorb – this results in nutritional deficiencies for the female and may also press on her lungs until she suffocates to death. Another name for this condition is egg retention.

They key to identifying an egg bound female is to know when to expect her to lay eggs. An egg-carrying female will likely stop eating when she is getting ready to deposit her eggs and she will likely start scratching at the ground and walls of the cage to dig a nest. If no proper nesting materials are available, the female may become egg bound as a result of refusing to lay the eggs. To prevent this, provide your gravid female with a deep, sandy enclosure in which to lay her eggs. Symptoms of egg binding include difficulty breathing, open mouth breathing, anorexia and inability to climb. Egg binding is incredibly serious and requires veterinary care to prevent it from becoming fatal.

Intestinal Parasites

Though many parasites have the capacity to infect veiled chameleons, the two most commonly seen in this species are pinworms and coccidia. Wild-caught chameleons are more likely than captive-bred specimens to be carrying parasites, but even captive-bred lizards can be exposed to parasites through contaminated food or feces. Parasite infections can only be diagnosed by a veterinarian through testing of the fecal matter.

The most common sign of intestinal parasites is a change in fecal matter – this may include diarrhea or loose stools, bloody stool, undigested food, or foul-smelling stools. After diagnosis by a veterinarian to identify the type of parasite causing the infection, your veiled chameleon will likely require treatment with anti-parasitic medications. Even if your chameleon seems fine, periodic fecal exams are recommended – especially if you include wild insects in your chameleon's diet. Other potential sources of contamination include water sources, contact with other reptiles, and poor hygiene.

Kidney Failure

Unfortunately, kidney failure is a fairly common occurrence (and a common cause of death) in captive chameleons. The main cause for kidney failure is chronic low-level dehydration. Kidney failure may also be brought on by the use of certain nephrotoxic antibiotics such as Amikacin which are used to treat certain bacterial infections. If your veterinarian prescribes antibiotics for your chameleon, make sure you ask him about the possibility of kidney failure or toxic reactions to the medication.

Some common signs of kidney failure in chameleons include swelling in the joints, dangling of one or more legs while perching, pain in movement, and gout. X-rays and blood tests are the usual means of diagnosis for kidney failure and they can only be performed by a qualified veterinarian. These tests will also help to rule out the possibility of injury being the cause for the symptoms. The most important part of treatment for this condition is rehydrating the chameleon and keeping it alive long enough for it to heal.

Metabolic Bone Disease

One of the most common (and deadly) diseases seen in captive reptiles like the veiled chameleon in metabolic bone disease (MBD). This disease is the result of a nutritional deficiency – specifically, inadequate amounts of calcium, phosphorus, vitamin A, and vitamin D3 in the diet. Though MBD is most commonly seen in juvenile chameleons, it can affect chameleons at any age if their diet does not provide adequate nutrition. Perhaps the most dangerous thing about this disease is that it acts slowly, progressing over time to a point where the damage may be irreversible by the time you notice the symptoms.

Common symptoms of metabolic bone disease include thinning or bending of the bones, frequent fractures or breaks, rubbery jaw bone, kinked tail or spine, difficulty moving quickly and unsteadiness. In the late stages of the disease, the chameleon may be too weak to perch on a branch and may not be able to project its tongue in order to eat or drink. The key to treating this disease is to supplement the chameleon's diet with the necessary vitamins and minerals. Exposure to natural sunlight or UVB light will help the chameleon to absorb necessary nutrients more effectively as well.

Respiratory Infection

Upper respiratory infections are fairly common in captive chameleons and they are most often the result of poor husbandry or improper caging. In many cases, respiratory infections are brought on by low temperatures or stagnant air in the cage, but it can also be caused by dirty bedding or contaminated feeder insects. For the most part, respiratory infections are caused by bacteria that attacks the sinuses or respiratory tract though, in some cases, they can enter the lungs and lead to pneumonia.

Common symptoms of respiratory infections in veiled chameleons include gaping of the mouth, excess mucus in the mouth, raspy exhalations, wheezing, inflammation around the nostrils, and bubbling at the mouth and nostrils (in very advanced cases). In the early stages of respiratory infections, the symptoms can be subtle and easy to miss but, as the disease progresses, they become more severe and noticeable. Common treatments for respiratory infections include increasing the cage temperature and improving humidity levels as well as administration of antibiotic medications.

Stomatitis

Also known as chameleon mouth disease, stomatitis is an infection affecting the mouth, tongue and esophagus. This disease has several potential causes including bacterial infection and poor nutrition. Poor temperature regulation, improper humidity levels, overcrowding, and various vitamin or mineral deficiencies may also contribute to the development of the disease. A blood test or sample of the chameleon's mucus will be enough to diagnose this condition.

Some common signs of stomatitis in veiled chameleons include staining along the gum line or the formation of brown or yellow matter around the mouth and teeth. Swelling of the jaw may also occur which may eventually affect the chameleon's interest in and ability to eat. If this infection goes untreated, it may cause permanent damage to the jaw bone. In severe cases, treatment may require surgical removal of the infected teeth or bone but, in mild cases, treatment with antibiotics (either topically or by injection) is sufficient. Keeping the chameleon warm and hydrated is important during the recovery period.

Stress

For chameleons kept in captivity, stress is fairly common. Unfortunately, chronic stress can be a very severe problem for chameleons, leading to a variety of dangerous (and potentially fatal) health problems. Unrelieved stress can depress the chameleon's immune system, leaving it more susceptible to infections and other illnesses. Below you will find tips for relieving/reducing stress for your veiled chameleon:

- Keep the cage in an area that receives little to no traffic – they can become stressed by noise and activity
- Make sure there is nothing in your chameleon's cage where he can see his reflection – he is likely to think it is another rival chameleon
- Never house more than one veiled chameleon in the same cage and keep the cage out of sight of other pets
- Do not force your chameleon to interact if he is displaying defensive behaviors
- Make sure that your chameleon's cage is large enough – if he doesn't have adequate room to move around he will become stressed

2.) Preventing Illness

Even if your veiled chameleon doesn't come down with a disease, there are many ways in which you may find him in less than top condition. In this section you will receive some practical tips for ensuring that your veiled chameleon gets what he needs to be as healthy as possible.

Below you will find tips for preventing illness in your veiled chameleons:

- Give your chameleon time outdoors, when the temperature is warm enough, to ensure that he gets enough vitamin D in his diet – while UVB lights in the cage will help to ensure proper absorption of nutrients, a little sunlight goes a long way

- Keeping the humidity in your chameleon's cage within the proper range will not only help to keep him hydrated, but it will also ensure that he is less likely to become stressed as a result of inadequate living conditions

- Chameleons are ectothermic animals which means that they rely on the temperature of their environment to regulate their body temperatures – making sure your chameleon's cage is warm enough will ensure that his body temperature stays within the proper range so it functions correctly

- Gut-loading feeder insects and dusting them with reptile supplement powder will help to fill in the gaps in your chameleon's diet, ensuring that he gets enough vitamins and minerals to prevent deficiencies

- In addition to using supplements, you should also make sure to include as much variety as possible in your chameleon's diet – certain insects (like crickets) are high in protein while others (like wax worms) are high in fats, so a variety is necessary to round out your chameleon's diet

Chapter Eight: Veiled Chameleon Care Sheet

While this book is designed to provide you with all the basic information you need to get started as a veiled chameleon owner, you may have specific questions at times. When this happens, rather than flipping through the entire book to find what you need, simply refer to this handy care sheet. Here you will find summaries of facts for all the most important aspects of veiled chameleon care including basic information, feeding information, cage set-up tips and breeding facts.

1.) Basic Information

Scientific Name: *Chamaeleo calyptrus*

Classification: true chameleon, family Chamaeleonidae

Country of Origin: Yemen (also United Arab Emirates, Saudi Arabia)

Habitat: primarily in forested portions of the mountains

Diet: omnivorous, though primarily insectivorous

Size (male): 17 to 24 inches (43 to 61 cm) average

Size (female): 10 to 14 inches (25 to 35.5 cm)

Weight (male): 3.5 to 7 oz. (100 to 200 g)

Weight (female): 3.2 to 4.2 oz. (90 to 120 g)

Color (male): bright green with yellow, brown and blue spots/stripes

Color (female): overall green, some white markings; develop dark green color with blue/yellow spots when gravid

Unique Characteristics: casque on the head, prehensile tail, swiveling eyes

Sexual Dimorphism: males are larger and more colorful, have spurs on the back of the hind feet

Lifespan: average 7 years

2.) Habitat Requirements

Minimum Cage Dimensions (adult): 24x24x48 inches (61x61x122 cm)

Minimum Cage Dimensions (juvenile): 16x16x30 inches (40.6x40.6x72 cm)

Switching Cages: move to adult cage at 8 inches (20.3 cm)

Cage Options: mesh terrarium (preferred) or glass terrarium

Pros and Cons: mesh terrarium facilitates air flow, reduces risk for fungal and respiratory infections; glass terrarium keeps cage warmer in cold climates

Lighting Types: use both heat lamps and UVB bulbs

Amount of Light: 10 to 12 hours per day UVB exposure

Ambient Temperature (daytime): 80° to 90°F (26° to 32°C)

Ambient Temperature (nighttime): drop by about 10° to 15°F (5° to 10°C)

Basking Temperature: 95°F (35°C)

Basking Area: position a perch 6 to 8 inches (15 to 20 cm) below heat lamp

Decorations: live plants, plastic plants, branches, vines

Live Plants: ficus, hibiscus, pothos, dracaena

Water: requires daily misting (at least twice per day)

Misting Options: automatic mister, spray bottle, bowl with air stone, dripping water source

3.) Nutritional Needs

Diet: omnivorous in the wild, primarily insectivorous in captivity

Preferred Insects: crickets, meal worms, waxworms, silkworms, moths, flies, locusts, roaches, butterworms, grasshoppers

Essential Vitamins/Minerals: calcium, phosphorus, vitamin A, vitamin D3

Supplements: calcium/vitamin D3 2 to 3 times weekly, broad vitamin/mineral supplement once a week

Feeding Insects: gut-load with fresh fruits and vegetables

Other Foods: fresh vegetables like greens, squash, zucchini, bell pepper and dandelion; fruits like apple and blueberries

Frequency of Feeding: constant or daily for juveniles; 3 to 4 times weekly for adults

Amount to Feed: as much as they can consume in 30-45 minutes

4.) Breeding Tips

Breeding Type: oviparous (egg laying)

Sexual Maturity (age): 4 to 5 months

Sexual Maturity (size): 8 to 12 inches (20 to 30.5 cm)

Breeding Frequency: up to 3 clutches per year

Breeding Indications: female changes color within 18 hours of a successful mating

Gestation Period: average 30 to 40 days

Eggs per Clutch: between 12 and 80, average 12 to 20

Nesting Box: 5-gallon (19 liter) bucket

Egg Laying Requirements: 6 to 12 inches (15 to 30.5 cm) warm sand or substrate

Days to Hatching: 150 to 200

Egg Appearance: white, oval shaped, tough skin

Incubation: plastic shoebox filled with Perlite or moist vermiculite

Egg Spacing: about 1 inch apart

Incubation Temperature (daytime): 75°F to 85°F (24° to 29°C)

Incubation Temperature (nighttime): 68°F (20°C)

Housing Hatchlings: 6 to 7 per 10-gallon (38-liter) tank

Feeding: pinhead crickets, as many as they will eat; dust with calcium supplement daily

Separation: separate the sexes at 2 months

Chapter Nine: Relevant Websites

Throughout this book you have received a wealth of information regarding the care and keeping of veiled chameleons. As you prepare to bring your own chameleons home, however, you may find that you need more information about a certain subject. In this chapter you will find a collection of relevant websites and resources to round out your education about veiled chameleons. Here you will find websites in the following categories: food, cages, supplies and general information.

1.) Food for Veiled Chameleons

In this section you will find resources for feeding veiled chameleon including websites to purchase food as well as information about feeding your chameleons.

United States Websites:

"Food and Diet." ChameleonCare.net. <http://chameleoncare.net/food-diet/>

"Feeder Crickets, Worms, Rodents, Roaches and More." LLLReptile. <http://www.lllreptile.com/catalog/106-feeder-crickets-worms-rodents-roaches-and-more>

"Chameleon Food." Chameleon Paradise. <http://www.chameleonparadise.net/information/chameleo n-food/>

Armstrong's Cricket Farm. <http://www.armstrongcrickets.com/crickets>

United Kingdom Websites:

"Feeding and Supplementation." Chameleonden.co.uk.
<http://www.chameleonden.co.uk/feeding.html>

"Caring for Feeder Insects." HadesDragons.co.uk.
<http://www.hadesdragons.co.uk/feeder.html>

LiveFoods Direct. <http://www.livefoodsdirect.co.uk/>

Livefood UK Ltd. <http://www.livefood.co.uk/>

2.) Cages for Veiled Chameleons

In this section you will find resources for veiled chameleon cages including websites to buy them and information about setting up your chameleon's cage.

United States Websites:

"Terrariums." Exo-Terra.com. <http://www.exo-terra.com/en/products/terrariums.php>

"Reptile Habitats." Doctors Foster and Smith. <http://www.drsfostersmith.com/reptile-supplies/reptile-habitats-homes-cages/ps/c/6016/6018>

Chappell, Sean. "How to Build Reptile Cages with Free Plans." eHow.com. <http://www.ehow.com/how_7781275_build-reptile-cages-plans.html?culture=en-US&redirect=%2Fhow_5101270_build-lizard-cage.html>

"Hybrid Reptile Cages." CagesbyDesign. <http://www.cagesbydesign.com/t-hybridreptile.aspx>

United Kingdom Websites:

"Reptile Terrariums and Vivariums." Seapets.co.uk.
<http://www.seapets.co.uk/products/reptile-
supplies/reptile-terrariums/>

"Housing – Mesh Vivariums." Blue Lizard Reptiles.
<http://www.bluelizardreptiles.co.uk/housing/meshvivariu
ms>

"Decoration – Terrarium and Vivarium Decoration."
888Reptiles. <http://www.888reptiles.co.uk/
productsubcategories.php?SubCategoryID=243>

"Enclosures/Habitat." Successful Keeping of Veiled
Chameleons.
<http://raisingkittytheveiledchameleon.blogspot.co.uk/2007/
12/enclosures-habitat.html?m=1>

3.) Supplies for Veiled Chameleons

In this section you will find resources for veiled chameleon supplies including cage accessories, basking rocks, heat lamps and more.

United States Websites:

"Cage Accessories." Kammerflage Kreations. <http://www.chameleonsonly.com/catalog/Cage_Accessories-7-1.html>

"Chameleon Supplies." Doctors Foster and Smith. <http://www.drsfostersmith.com/reptile-supplies/species-specific-reptile-products/chameleon-products/ps/c/6016/20175/19809>

"Chameleon Supplies." Amazon.com. <http://www.amazon.com/s/ref=nb_sb_noss_1?url=node%3D2975504011&field-keywords=chameleon>

United Kingdom Websites:

"Reptile Lighting – Bulbs." Blue Lizard Reptiles.
<http://www.bluelizardreptiles.co.uk/reptilelighting/bulbs>

"Reptile Lighting and UV Bulbs." PetsParade.co.uk.
<http://www.petsparade.co.uk/reptiles/lighting/>

"Heat Rocks for Reptiles." Seapets.co.uk.
<http://www.seapets.co.uk/products/reptile-supplies/reptile-equipment/reptile-heating/heat-rocks-for-reptiles/all-products.html>

Rainforest Reptile Supplies.
<http://www.rainforestsupplies.co.uk/lrf/index.php>

4.) General Info for Veiled Chameleons

In this section you will find an assortment of websites regarding general information and care for veiled chameleons as pets.

United States Websites:

"Types of Chameleons." ChameleonCare.net. <http://chameleoncare.net/types-of-chameleons/>

"Veiled Chameleon." LLL Reptile. <http://www.lllreptile.com/info/library/animal-care-sheets/chameleons/-/veiled-chameleon/>

"Veiled Chameleon." Petco.com. <http://www.petco.com/product/118276/Veiled-Chameleon.aspx>

"Veiled Chameleon Care Sheet." Veiled Chameleon Care Sheet. <http://www.veiledchameleoncaresheet.com/>

United Kingdom Websites:

"Successful Keeping of Veiled Chameleons." Raising Kitty the Veiled Chameleon. <http://raisingkittytheveiledchameleon.blogspot.co.uk/2007/12/keeping-female-veiled.html?m=1>

"Veiled Chameleon Care Sheet." UK Chameleons. <http://www.martinsreptiles.co.uk/ukchams/calyptratus_caresheet.htm>

"Yemen/Veiled Chameleon." TC Reptiles. <http://www.tcreptiles.co.uk/veiledchameleoncare.htm>

"Veiled Chameleon Care Sheet." TheReptilian.co.uk. <http://www.thereptilian.co.uk/care_sheets/veiled_chameleon_yemen_chameleon_Chamaeleo_calyptratus_care_sheet.htm>

Index

D

E

F

G

H

M

N

O

T

U

V

W

Photo Credits

Cover Photo By Flickr user Udo Schroter, <https://www.flickr.com/photos/nordelch/286985229/sizes/l

Page 1 Photo By Geoff via Wikimedia Commons, <http://en.wikipedia.org/wiki/Veiled_chameleon#mediavie wer/File:C_Calyptratus_female.jpg>

Page 6 Photo By Steven G. Johnson, via Wikimedia Commons, <http://commons.wikimedia.org/wiki/ File:Veiled_chameleon,_Boston.jpg>

Page 15 Photo By Gilles Moynot via Wikimedia Commons, <http://commons.wikimedia.org/wiki/File:Furcifer_lateralis. JPG>

Page 16 Photo By Ales.Kocourek via Wikimedia Commons, <http://en.wikipedia.org/wiki/File:Chameleon_-_Tanzania_-_Usambara_Mountains.jpg>

Page 17 Photo By Movingsaletoday via Wikimedia Commons,

<http://commons.wikimedia.org/wiki/File:Jackson%27s_Ch
ameleon_2_edit1.jpg>

Page 18 Photo By Adrian Pingstone via Wikimedia
Commons, <http://en.wikipedia.org/wiki/
File:Mellers.chameleon.bristol.zoo.arp.jpg>

Page 19 Photo By Charlesjsharp via Wikimedia Commons,
<http://en.wikipedia.org/wiki/File:Oustalet%27s_chameleon
_furcifer_oustaleti_female.jpg>

Page 20 Photo By Marc Staub via Wikimedia Commons,
<http://en.wikipedia.org/wiki/File:Furcifer_pardalis_-
Z%C3%BCrich_Zoo-8a.jpg>

Page 21 Photo By Jarek Tuszynski via Wikimedia
Commons,
<http://commons.wikimedia.org/wiki/File:Washington_DC_
Zoo_-_Veiled_Chameleon_4.jpg>

Page 26 Photo By H. Zell via Wikimedia Commons,
<http://commons.wikimedia.org/wiki/File:Chamaeleo_calyp
tratus_01.jpg>

Page 36 Photo By Chiswick Chap via Wikimedia Commons, <http://commons.wikimedia.org/wiki/File:Yemen_Chameleon_(cropped).jpg>

Page 41 Photo By Flickr user LaertesCTB, <https://www.flickr.com/photos/laertes_za/3055819486/sizes/l>

Page 46 Photo By Matt Reinhold via Wikimedia Commons, <http://commons.wikimedia.org/wiki/File:Chamaeleo_calyptratus1.jpg>

Page 50 Photo By Norbert Sdunzik via Wikimedia Commons, <http://commons.wikimedia.org/wiki/File:Jemencham%C3%A4leon_Chamaeleo_calyptratus.jpg>

Page 56 Photo By OpenCage.info, <http://opencage.info/pics/large_16055.asp>

Page 59 Photo By OpenCage.info, <http://opencage.info/pics.e/large_15953.asp>

Page 66 Photo By Jarek Tuszynski via Wikimedia Commons, <http://commons.wikimedia.org/wiki/File:Washington_DC_Zoo_-_Veiled_Chameleon_1.jpg>

Page 80 Photo By OpenCage.info, <http://opencage.info/pics.e/large_15971.asp>

Page 86 Photo By OpenCage.info, <http://opencage.info/pics/large_15958.asp>

References

"Average Cost of Owning a Chameleon." Much Ado About Chameleons.
<http://muchadoaboutchameleons.blogspot.com/2012/03/average-cost-of-owning-chameleon.html>

"Bacterial Diseases of Reptiles." Merck Manual Veterinary Edition. <http://www.merckmanuals.com/vet/exotic_and_laboratory_animals/reptiles/bacterial_diseases_of_reptiles.html>

"Captive Reptile & Amphibian Permit/License." Maryland Department of Natural Resources.
<http://www.dnr.state.md.us/wildlife/Licenses/captive.asp>

Casselman, Anne. "Chameleons Evolved Color Changing to Communicate." National Geographic News.
<http://news.nationalgeographic.com/news/2008/01/080128-chameleon-color.html>

Davis, Jen. "How to Identify an Egg Bound Chameleon." PawNation Animals. <http://animals.pawnation.com/ identify-egg-bound-chameleon-4354.html>

"Fact Sheets – Veiled Chameleon." Smithsonian National Zoological Park. <http://nationalzoo.si.edu/animals/ reptilesamphibians/facts/factsheets/veiledchameleon.cfm>

"Handling Your Chameleon." Chameleon World. <http://chamworld.blogspot.com/2008/01/handling-your-chameleon.html>

Johnston, Dave. "The Costs of Keeping Chameleons." Chameleon News. <http://www.chameleonnews.com/ 03JulJohnston.html>

McLeod, Lianne. "Choosing a Pet Chameleon." AboutHome. <http://exoticpets.about.com/od/chameleons/ qt/choosecham.htm>

"Metabolic Bone Disease (MBD)." ChameleonDen.co.uk. <http://www.chameleonden.co.uk/metabolic.html>

"Reptile Glossary of Terms." Animal-World Encyclopedia.
< http://animal-world.com/encyclo/reptiles/information/
reptile_glossary.php>

"Reptile Keeper's License." NSW Environment and
Heritage. <http://www.environment.nsw.gov.au/
wildlifelicences/ReptileKeepersLicence.htm>

"Selecting a Healthy Chameleon." ChameleonDen.co.uk.
<http://www.chameleonden.co.uk/selecting.html>

"Signs of Trouble." Animal Ark Shelter.
<http://www.animalarkshelter.org/animal/CIN/ContentMg
mt.nsf/Trouble/$first?OpenDocument>

Spiess, Petra. "Breeding the Veiled Chameleon."
Kingsnake.com. <http://www.kingsnake.com/
rockymountain/RMHPages/RMHCarpets.htm>

"Types of Chameleons." ChameleonCare.net.
<http://chameleoncare.net/types-of-chameleons/>

"Veiled Chameleon." LLL Reptile. <http://www.lllreptile.com/info/library/animal-care-sheets/chameleons/-/veiled-chameleon/>

"Veiled Chameleon." Petco.com. <http://www.petco.com/product/118276/Veiled-Chameleon.aspx>

"Veiled Chameleons." PetSuppliesPlus. <http://www.petsuppliesplus.com/content.jsp?pageName=veiled_chameleons>

"Veiled Chameleon Care Sheet." Veiled Chameleon Care Sheet. <http://www.veiledchameleoncaresheet.com/>

"What are the Pros and Cons of a Chameleon as a Pet?" WiseGeek.org. <http://www.wisegeek.org/what-are-the-pros-and-cons-of-a-chameleon-as-a-pet.htm>

CPSIA information can be obtained
at www.ICGtesting.com
Printed in the USA
BVOW10s0531231116

468704BV00008B/140/P